mourad
new moroccan

mourad
new moroccan

mourad lahlou

With Susie Heller, Steve Siegelman, and Amy Vogler
Photographs by Deborah Jones

ARTISAN

Published by Artisan
A division of
Workman Publishing Company, Inc.
225 Varick Street
New York, NY 10014-4381
artisanbooks.com

Published simultaneously in Canada
by Thomas Allen & Son, Limited

Library of Congress
Cataloging-in-Publication Data
Lahlou, Mourad.
Mourad : new Moroccan / Mourad Lahlou ; with Susie Heller,
Steve Siegelman, and Amy Vogler ; photographs by Deborah Jones.
p. cm.
Includes index.
ISBN 978-1-57965-429-0
1. Cooking, Moroccan. 2. Cookbooks. I. Title.
TX725.M8L34 2011
641.5964—dc22
2011005682

Design by i4 design, Sausalito, CA

Printed in Singapore

10 9 8 7 6 5 4 3 2

To my grandpa, Hajj Ben Seddiq,
still and always, my loving guide,
my voice, my values,
the barometer of my soul,
and the true author of my story

CONTENTS

cooking from memory

Some people set out to learn to cook. They pursue it. They look for teachers. They go to cooking school. They practice and study. I became a cook in a way that could scarcely have been more different from all of that, in a place so far from where I ended up that it feels like a beautiful, brightly colored dream. I learned to cook from memory. Let me tell you how.

I was born in Casablanca. That's where my dad was from, and my mom had moved there from her native Marrakesh to marry him. But that marriage didn't last, and when my parents split up just a few months after I came along, my mom took my brother and me back to her family home—a twenty-room maze of a building on a crooked street in the ancient medina of Marrakesh. From that moment on, my dad vanished from our lives forever, but something else took his place.

In Morocco, family is everything. The idea of a kid growing up with only one parent isn't just a sad matter to cluck your tongue at. It's thought of as a tragedy, and when it happens, people tend to overcompensate. I lost a dad, but when we moved into that beehive of a house, I gained a dozen parents—my uncles, aunts, great-grandmother, grandmother, and grandfather—who showered me with attention, love, and praise. And food.

Like most traditional Moroccan houses, ours had two floors, with no windows on the ground floor for privacy. We were neither rich nor poor, but, rather, perfectly comfortable in the sprawling complex that had been in our family for generations and always had a place for whoever needed it. It was built around a light-filled courtyard overlooked by colonnaded balconies, with a large lemon tree in the middle. Upstairs, the bedrooms were grouped somewhat randomly into apartments. Downstairs were three big rooms that opened onto the courtyard: a salon for receiving guests, a family room with a gigantic round table where we ate every meal, and, largest of all, the kitchen.

The kitchen was the spiritual center of the place, but it was all business. Its walls were whitewashed and for the most part unadorned, with a few simple decorations breaking up the expanse: a century-old tagine, now too precious and fragile to use; some rustic spoons hanging from nails; and a photo of a long-gone great-grandmother. A propane stove, a refrigerator, a sink, and a terra-cotta charcoal brazier took up one wall. There were no counters or cupboards, only a couple of shelves to hold pots, pans, spices, and staples.

The real action took place in the middle of the room, at a low round table flanked by a few mismatched chairs. No one ever sat down to eat there. It was the prep table, where the women of the house would sit for hours, working and talking.

From the time I can remember, every day began in exactly the same way. My mom, grandma, some of the aunts, my nanny, and a couple of other women who helped out around the house would get up early and head for the kitchen. Each had her own specialty, and they'd fall sleepily into their morning routine, preparing breakfast, doing laundry, and getting ready for the day ahead without much conversation.

One of them would make the bread for the day, proofing the dough, punching it down, forming it into eight big round loaves, and setting them to proof again on a long board for someone in the family to drop off at the bakery on the way to work or school.

As we stumbled downstairs one by one, we'd head to the family room for breakfast. There would be coffee (really more like warm milk with a little coffee in it), bread and olive oil, some kind of porridge, maybe a little leftover *harira*—Morocco's much-loved lentil and tomato soup—or fried eggs with strips of the aged beef called *khlea,* or perhaps some of my mom's famous *beghrir* pancakes.

And then, when we were all assembled, the ritual would begin. It was like a play that had been running at the same theater for years. A play about a family, with familiar characters and dialogue—the kind of play you could watch over and over, a melodrama with wringing of hands, laughter, and a comfortably predictable story line that always turned out right. It was called *What's for Lunch?*

In Morocco, as in much of the world, the midday meal is the main event of the day. Stores, businesses, and schools close at noon, and by 12:30, the entire country is sitting down to a national family meal. Like everywhere else, it's a tradition that's eroding, but in the early '70s, it was still an absolute rule.

I would sit on a small chair near the table and watch the characters in our little daily production run through their lines and their choreography—voices rising with emotion, hands slapping the table, arms folding resolutely over chests.

GRANDPA: *Sidi Ibrahim has very fine okra now.*

GRANDMA: *Okra! We had it yesterday. And the day before. And the day before that. And also last Tuesday. I'm tired of it. I never liked it to begin with. Okra.*

GRANDPA: *Ah. How is it you never mentioned this before? Me, when it's in season, I could eat it every day. And anyway, next week it will be gone. No more okra.* [Clapping his hands silently] *We could have it with* [dramatic pause] *lamb.*

ONE OF THE AUNTS (the one with the big job in the fancy office): *Please. No lamb. Something lighter that won't make us all fat and sleepy! I can't eat like that every day.*

GRANDMA: *You want bland? That's fine. Eat bland.*

AN UNCLE (the one who has something to do with running the country's railroads): *Chicken, then? The one braised with saffron and crushed tomatoes and okra? Chicken is lighter.*

MY MOM: *Not if it's that chicken, it isn't. No, we'll make rice with eggplant.*

A PLUMP OLD AUNT: *You scrawny girls with your light food! How are you going to get a man with no meat on your bones?*

ANOTHER UNCLE (the schoolteacher): *Rice is a bore.*

GRANDMA: *All right. Rice then. But no eggplant. And definitely no okra!*

The grown-ups would argue like this for almost an hour. The kids never said a word, but not for lack of interest—at least on my part. My eyes would dart from person to person as I took it all in, learning what it meant to have real, heartfelt convictions about food and life. I could have sat there and listened all day.

At nine o'clock, Act 1 of our little breakfast-room drama came to an abrupt conclusion as Grandpa pushed his chair back loudly, grabbed a large straw shopping bag from the back of the door, took my hand, and led me through the courtyard and out onto the street.

Act 2 found us walking through the winding back alleys toward the market.

"So . . . what are we going to buy, *Abba*?" I would ask, already knowing the answer.

"Okra. And some nice lamb!"

And, from the time I was about four years old, this all made perfect sense to me: the ritual of the morning discussion and debate, in which everyone truly believed, day after day, that they had a vote on the day's menu; and the inevitable outcome—the menu my grandfather had in mind all along. I know it sounds paradoxical (or like a benevolent dictatorship, where the ruling patriarch simply laid down the law), but I also know now that the reason it made perfect sense to all of us was that the debate was actually an essential part of the cooking process. It was like a recipe that begins, "Spread out the ingredients on the table and argue over them for one hour before making the stew." That morning discussion was like a marinade that woke up appetites, got mouths watering, and set in motion the nuances and variations that would make that day's meal special. Grandpa, my first role model and my lifelong idol, wasn't a dictator. He was an executive chef.

Grandpa's morning route never varied. Seven days a week, first the meat, then the produce market. Along the way, he'd stop at all the same shops and greet the same merchants in the same way. And all through my childhood, on weekends, holidays, and throughout the summer, if I didn't have school, I'd never miss the chance to go along with him.

My grandfather, Hajj Ben Seddiq, ran a successful textile business (he bought, reprocessed, and sold wool and silk), and he was always impeccably dressed. His manner commanded respect, and he was revered throughout the city. He was confident and kind, with a sort of natural authority that allowed him to talk comfortably to everyone, young or old, rich or poor.

"I told you yesterday! Don't kick the ball that way—you'll wreck your shoes," he'd yell to a kid in the street, a grin betraying his serious tone. As we approached the market, he'd greet each vendor: "It's a beautiful day today. How is your lovely wife? Wasn't that a fine cup of tea we had yesterday? Is your cousin feeling better?"

Like the breakfast debate, it was all about ritual. He'd ask the exact same questions, like a man running through his daily prayers, as if the answers might have changed since the last time he'd asked, twenty-four hours earlier. I was mesmerized by every interaction. I didn't know it at the time, but I was learning how to be a human being.

We'd progress at a leisurely pace, doing more socializing than shopping. And all along the way, Grandpa would give me little treats—a stick of gum, a single square broken from a big bar of chocolate he kept in his pocket just for me, or half of a dry, skinny Deglet Noor date, always making me promise I wouldn't tell my mom how much he spoiled me.

As Grandpa tapped melons, smelled tomatoes, and examined the stems of the cumin for clues about freshness and flavor, I rarely asked questions, but, as it turns out, I was recording the whole thing in my mind for later review. And our treasure hunts in the market added up to a lifelong appreciation of raw materials and their possibilities.

"Come on," he would say over and over. "It'll be our own place. A place to hang out. Like Mamounia, but you can do the food even better."

I was still planning to become an economist and work for the World Bank or the IMF. But, just like when I was supposed to head to France for college, I had a little moment of doubt—an urge to rebel. So I agreed to a compromise. I told Khalid I'd do it for six months. Just long enough to help him find a location and get the kitchen going. And then I'd go back to my PhD plan. Fourteen years later, I'm still in the kitchen.

When Mamounia's branch in San Rafael, across the Golden Gate Bridge in Marin County, closed, we knew we'd found our spot. We borrowed money on a dozen credit cards and, with a little help from Saïd (and some leftover chairs from Mamounia), we opened Kasbah. The name says it all. We stuck with the Arabian Nights approach—the tented rooms, the belly dancers. But the place had a hipper vibe that everyone loved. You could tell young people had started it.

Our opening menu was a version of the familiar restaurant standbys. But after the initial frenzy of opening died down, I started to really focus on the food—on how to make it better.

In Mamounia's heyday, there had been one cook in the kitchen, serving two hundred or more meals a night. One guy! The menu had been carefully engineered to include slow-cooked and sturdy items that could be held on steam tables all evening, so when an order came in, no matter what it was, it could be quickly plated, sauced, garnished, and sent out by that single, lonely cook.

For some Moroccan dishes, that's just fine. But for others, it's a crime. I started cooking the vegetables for less time in the tagines, refining the presentations, cleaning up the flavors of that canon of tried-and-true dishes, cutting back on the spices, and reworking everything to be a little lighter and more carefully finished *à la minute*. And I started introducing more and more of the home-style dishes I had grown up with.

Kasbah was a big hit. The *San Francisco Chronicle* gave us three stars right away, and pretty soon the major food magazines were writing about us. Star Chefs named me a "Rising Star." And I discovered that I had turned a lifetime of memories into a career.

Five years later, our lease ran out, and we found a new location in San Francisco. I wanted to keep evolving, so I decided not to call the place Kasbah. (Besides, there was already a San Francisco strip joint with that name.) So I settled on Mosaic. We put up the sign and printed the menus. But a few days before we opened, my mom had a heart attack. Don't worry—she survived and is very much alive. But that day, we hastily changed the name of the restaurant to honor her. We called it Aziza.

Once again, we were a hit. The *Chronicle* gave us three stars, and the media and our loyal customers have echoed that enthusiasm ever since.

I never set out to be a chef. And I used to say that I just kind of stumbled into it. But I've finally figured out that it really wasn't an accident at all. When I look back on those years in Marrakesh, and think about that little boy watching that same play every day with endless fascination, it occurs to me that what I've done here, half a world away, is to re-create that play. Just like in that big kitchen of my childhood, I'm never alone at the restaurant. I'm surrounded by cooks all working to get the day's big meal ready. One person's chopping turnips, another is peeling carrots. Gossiping while they prep. Talking about food. And then getting quiet, intense, and serious as the big push to get the meal on the table approaches. Just like old times.

And the memories of my grandparents, my mom, and all those loud, wonderful women surround me too. I hear myself talking to my cooks. "When is it done? When is it *done?!* I don't know when it's done. Taste it! It's done when it *tastes good!*" I can even hear the pitch of my voice rising on the last words, like my mom, like my aunts.

Fortunately, for balance, I channel my grandpa too. He showed me a gentle way to be at peace with people and wish them well. On Saturday, July 29, 1999, my family called me from Marrakesh to tell me the sad news that he had died. I hung up the phone, and I shaved off every hair on my head, so I would never forget that day—and I never have.

Taking charge of memories in that way means a lot to me. When I go back to Morocco, I'm acutely aware that the dream world of my childhood no longer exists. The big family house stands empty, crumbling. Although everyone moved to the new part of town years ago, no one can bear to sell the old place. But the thing is, I don't long for that world. I cherish it, and I cook from it every day. And so, dish by dish, and year by year, my food evolves. I started at Kasbah with a somewhat obsessive attitude about showing people *real* Moroccan food, done the *authentic* way. But there we were in California. It's just not possible. The ingredients are all different—even the ones flown from Morocco don't taste the same by the time they arrive. There's no market to walk to with Grandpa.

So, before long, I was doing the Moroccan version of what so many inventive northern California chefs have done. I adapted what I knew and loved to make it work with the beautiful ingredients I can get here, and then just followed my nose, my heart, and my palate.

And that's what this book is about: my personal interpretation of Moroccan food. Some of it is actually very close to what you'd find in Morocco. The rest is the best of my riffing, improvisation, and culinary daydreaming over the years.

One image comes to mind that sums all this up. It's that sprawling lemon tree in the courtyard of our house in Marrakesh. I think of my food as that tree. Its deep roots are in Morocco—that's my inspiration. But as the tree grows, the buds appear, and the leaves reach up to the light, new things keep happening.

Cut off too many branches, and a tree will die. Let it grow wild, though, and one day, it will collapse under its own weight. So my way of cooking and culinary exploration is really a kind of pruning—constantly adjusting and adapting, welcoming new ways and fresh ideas, and always tending my tree with love.

before you start

Let me tell you why I wrote this book. It wasn't because I thought the world needed another Moroccan cookbook with essential classic recipes. And it wasn't because I'm looking to evolve Moroccan cuisine or take it someplace it doesn't want to go. I think of what I do as evolving *my* cuisine, and that's what this book is really about.

I've spent my entire adult life working with flavors and ideas from the Moroccan kitchen in ways that fit the way I like to cook in northern California, with a whole world of incredible ingredients at hand. Over the last two decades, that kind of experiment has added up to a very personal cuisine, and *that's* what I want to share with you. Some of the recipes in this book are dishes we serve or have served at Aziza. Others were inspired by that food or by food I remember from my childhood. They've all been adapted to work well in home kitchens.

My hope is that by getting a feel for the bigger ideas that make food Moroccan—the ingredients, the traditions, the ways of adding flavor—you can use them to evolve your own personal style of cooking, informed by what's cool, exciting, and soul-satisfying about Moroccan food, whether you're a curious home cook or a professional chef.

I've included "Chef to Chef" notes here and there, where I want to share ideas best suited to professionals or serious home cooks. I hope that whether or not you try them, you'll have fun reading them as glimpses into a kind of thinking most cookbooks don't include.

What follows here are some basic tools, ingredients, and techniques I think you'll find helpful.

General Notes

- We used high-quality cookware when testing the recipes, and I recommend you do the same, because lower-grade pots and pans can burn food or cook it unevenly. For these recipes, a good set of cookware would include traditional and nonstick frying pans, a Dutch oven (preferably enameled), and a heavy cast-iron skillet for searing.
- A good, strong blender (I recommend a Vita-Mix) will make a big difference in preparing many of these recipes, giving you very smooth purees, soups, and sauces with much less waste when you strain them.
- There are many factors that determine cooking times, from the stove to the cookware, the ingredients, and even the weather—so use your judgment, trust your instincts and your senses, and make adjustments accordingly.

Sources

The recipes in this book call for a fair number of unusual ingredients or cookware, but we chose to not interrupt the flow of the recipes by constantly referring you to the Sources section on page 380. Rest assured, though, that we've included Internet and retail sources there for everything you'll need.

Weighing and Measuring

I give both volume (i.e., teaspoons, cups, etc.) and weight (metric) measurements throughout the book. In my kitchen, I measure ingredients exclusively by weight, using gram scales, and I encourage you to do the same for several reasons.

◆ *Weight is more accurate than volume.* If you don't believe me, measure a tablespoon of kosher salt. It will weigh about 9 grams. Now fold the salt up in a piece of parchment and smash it with a rolling pin. Pour it back into the tablespoon, and you'll see that its volume is reduced by as much as third. But it's still 9 grams. Get the idea? Grams are grams whether you're measuring a liquid or a solid—whole, chopped, or crushed.

◆ *Scales are easier to use.* Say you're using a dozen liquid and dry ingredients for a sauce. You put a bowl on the scale, zero it out, add the first ingredient, zero it again, and repeat, zeroing each time. You'll end up dirtying only a single bowl instead of a bowl and a whole set of measuring implements. (Just be sure to add each ingredient gradually, because if you go over the weight you need, that's not an easy mistake to undo.)

◆ *Grams are more precise.* With grams, there's no need for rounding. You can easily, accurately weigh out 0.6 grams of something, for example, whereas ¼ teaspoon of the same ingredient is, by definition, a somewhat approximate measurement that will vary a bit depending on who's eyeballing the measurement.

◆ *The metric system gives you a sense of proportion.* Rather than having to think in terms of teaspoons, cups, fluid ounces, ounces, and pounds, working in grams puts everything on the same footing, giving you an instant sense of proportions. It not only makes it easier to scale up or down, it also gives you a much better understanding of a recipe, just by scanning the ingredient list.

Convinced? Good. Invest in two digital scales: a small one that measures increments as small as ¹⁄₁₀₀ gram and a larger one that goes up to 5 kilos.

Note that for ingredients requiring extreme precision (such as spices and seasonings), I've rounded metric measurements off to the nearest tenth of a gram. For other ingredients, I've rounded to the nearest whole gram.

Ingredients

OILS

These days, a lot of home cooks seem to default to a single bottle of good olive oil as an all-purpose ingredient for cooking, dressings, and finishing. I recommend having a variety of oils on hand for different uses.

◆ *For searing and high-heat cooking,* use a neutral oil with a high smoke point. At the restaurant, I use rice bran oil and grapeseed oil. For home cooks, canola is a less expensive alternative. Don't waste extra virgin olive oil on this purpose; the heat will destroy its flavor.

- *For finishing vegetables,* I recommend a buttery, peppery extra virgin olive oil, such as De Padova Organic Extra Virgin made in Puglia.
- *For finishing meat,* try a milder, creamy extra virgin olive oil that won't mask the flavor of the meat. I like Del Monaco Organic Extra Virgin, from Calabria.
- *For finishing fish,* Mosto Oro from Calvi & Co. in Liguria is super-buttery but delicate enough to go perfectly with seafood.
- *For an all-purpose finishing oil,* Olivestri Siloro from Umbria is the one I'd take to a desert island. It's olivey yet delicate, creamy, and not the least bit bitter, so it goes with everything.
- *Also check out:* Olivestri Siloro Olio Nuovo (a very fresh, peppery new oil, available only in the fall, right after the olive harvest) and the rich, grassy organic Tuscan olive oils of Armando Manni.

The simpler the dish—say, Early Girl tomatoes with salt and olive oil—the more the oil becomes an essential component, and the more important its flavor is. Keep in mind that price is not always the best way to judge the quality of an olive oil. Like wine, the only real standard is your own palate. If you like how an oil tastes and the way it brings out the flavor of a dish, it's a good oil.

VINEGARS

I use a variety of vinegars with different degrees of acidity and flavors.

- I love two vinegars from Katz and Company: their Trio Red Wine Vinegar is a great all-purpose choice, and their Sparkling Wine (aka Champagne) Vinegar is a good choice for vinaigrettes.
- Aged sherry vinegar and aged balsamic are pricey but worth it. Use them for finishing dishes, so you get their full flavor. They'll be lost in most dressings and cooking uses.

SALTS

- For recipes that call for kosher salt, we used Diamond kosher salt in testing.
- For finishing dishes, I sprinkle on crunchy sea salt. I like flaky Maldon salt for cold foods. Maldon tends to melt quickly in hot foods, so there, I go with French fleur de sel.

WINE AND ALCOHOL

Yes, I cook with them, even though I don't drink them. Wine was not, of course, a part of my cultural or culinary upbringing in Morocco. I tasted it exactly once growing up and hated it. But here in California, it's not something I want to ignore, so over the years, I've learned to use wine and spirits in my food, always cooking off the alcohol.

ROSE WATER AND ORANGE BLOSSOM WATER

These fragrant waters, made by distilling rose petals or orange blossoms, are widely used in Moroccan food. Cortas, the brand of rose water that shows up in most supermarkets, is quite mild. Other higher-end brands are more concentrated, so use them sparingly at first, until you get a feel for their potency and flavor. You can generally use rose and orange blossom water interchangeably. Use just enough to add a light floral perfume in the background; if the flavor is instantly identifiable in the finished dish, you've probably gone too far.

CAPERS

Salt-packed capers and caper berries are much tastier than the brined kind. To use the salt-packed ones, soak them in 3 or 4 changes of water for a total of about half an hour. They'll still be fairly salty, but the soaking will reduce the salt enough to bring out a lot more of their flavor. In some recipes, especially ones that call for herbs crushed in a mortar, try crushing capers in the same way and using them as a seasoning in place of salt.

CITRIC ACID

For times when you want to add sourness but don't want to add a liquid (say, in a spice blend or a dry rub), citric acid is incredibly useful. It's a white powder, naturally derived from citrus and other acidic fruits, that's inexpensive and commonly available in the canning section of grocery stores. Just remember that a little goes a long way, so start with a small amount until you get used to working with it.

XANTHAN GUM AND LECITHIN

I use both of these emulsifiers in my cooking. Even though they might sound like strange chemical additives, both are naturally produced and won't affect the flavor of food when used in the right proportions. Lecithin is great when you're making a foam and you want to give it body and holding power. Xanthan gum thickens sauces, purees, and dressings without cooking, giving them a nice sheen and firmer texture. I often add it to dressings to keep them emulsified. Using either lecithin and xanthan gum is a pretty exact science, in the sense that a small amount is all you need, and adding too much can cause them to backfire and produce a weird consistency you don't want. But I encourage you to look for them (in well-stocked health foods markets or grocery stores) and give them a try.

MEAT

For best flavor and texture, I recommend buying red meat 3 to 4 days ahead of time so you can dry-age it. To do this, pat the meat dry, wrap it in a single layer of cheesecloth, and set it on a baking sheet in the coldest part of your refrigerator. You'll need to change the cheesecloth if it gets saturated. I also recommend salting and seasoning meat the day before you plan to use it. This is a kind of "dry brining" technique that draws flavor into the meat. (It's a myth, by the way, that salting meat before you cook it keeps it from searing or browning well.)

seven things

The number seven is sacred in Morocco, especially when it comes to food. Meals begin with seven salads. Couscous is topped with seven vegetables. And for me, it's a number that just feels right. So I decided to begin this book with seven things that really matter to me about Moroccan cooking and *my* cooking. I've structured them as seven little "classes" with master recipes. I hope you'll read them before you start cooking from this book, and that you'll actually cook your way through them too. If you do, your kitchen will be stocked with some wonderful seasoning and cooking essentials, and you'll have a much better sense of where I'm coming from—and where I want to take you.

spice is a verb

1

"It's all about the spices, right?" That's usually the first question I hear whenever I talk about Moroccan cooking. And the answer is "No. It's really all about what you do with them."

Look, the six most used spices in Moroccan cooking are cumin, ginger, coriander, turmeric, white pepper, and paprika. I'll bet you have a jar of each of them sitting in your cupboard right now.

You probably also have most of the other common ones:

cinnamon, allspice, nutmeg, cayenne, and mustard seeds, and maybe even some saffron, star anise, and cardamom.

But here's the thing. I'm guessing you bought some of those spices for a Mexican recipe, some to add to a curry, and others for making a Thanksgiving dessert. After all, ever since the Egyptians started trading spices four thousand years ago, the major spice players have found their way into most of the world's great cuisines, and somewhere along the way, most of them have passed through the strategically located trading hub that is Morocco. So it's not the spices themselves that make Moroccan food taste and smell Moroccan. There really aren't *Moroccan* spices. There are the great spices of the world. And Moroccan cooking is about how they're treated, combined, and cooked.

Spices have a weird, magical quality that I can't resist. They smell wonderful, but put them on your tongue and you're likely to find them bitter and off-putting. The magic comes in how you coax out their essential flavors and get them to mellow and harmonize with one another and with the other ingredients in a dish. That harmony is what you experience when you're sitting around a big round table in Morocco and an enormous lidded platter is brought out. The lid comes off, and the hypnotic blend of aromas makes you hungry and curious, even if you've tasted the dish a thousand times.

My work in the kitchen over the last twenty years has largely been about studying and understanding that magic effect and gradually—through practice and playing around, through trial and error—mastering the main instruments in the orchestra of Moroccan spices so I can use them to make my own music.

Spice and Sauce

A fundamental principle that distinguishes Moroccan cooking from other cuisines that might be more familiar to you (say French, Italian, Mexican, Spanish, or even Chinese) is that in Morocco, flavors aren't typically built on a foundation of searing meat, cooking aromatics in the rendered fat, deglazing the pan with stock or wine, and reducing the liquid. Moroccan cooking evolved around the use of clay vessels over coal fires, a braising technique that's not conducive to browning or searing.

Instead, the meat and vegetables are usually combined with spices right at the start, cooked for a bit to toast the spices, and then simmered with onions, water, and other ingredients. What that means is that you get lots of sauce, and its flavor comes *more from the spices than from the meat.*

This is how I remember those big platters that were the main event at every lunch of my childhood: the domed lid would be lifted, and you'd see sauce with vegetables piled in the middle, with a bit of meat hidden under them. Everyone would begin by eating bread with the sauce and then with vegetables as a way to fill up. The meat would be gradually uncovered and savored last, and if there were guests, they'd be offered the best pieces. It was rude—unheard of, really—to dig right into the meat or the vegetables. You always started with the sauce and worked your way in to the center. Even today, when traditional dishes are on the menu in Moroccan homes, that's still pretty much the rule. So the real soul of the meal is that abundant sauce. And the soul of that sauce is the spices.

Sweet and Savory

More than any cuisine I know, Moroccan food loves to play in the space between sweet and savory. Sugar and honey are used abundantly in savory dishes, along with dates, prunes, and other fruit, and it's impossible to talk about the role of spices in the cuisine without putting them in the context of this sweet-savory balance.

Think about what gives a spice cake its flavor: cinnamon, clove, allspice, nutmeg, and mace. Those sweet spices have a natural affinity for sugar, caramel, and dried fruit. In Moroccan cooking, that affinity is exploited not in desserts (which scarcely exist as part of a traditional meal), but in savory dishes, especially stews and braises made with beef and lamb. Braised lamb shank with prunes and honey is a classic example of how sweet spices and ingredients marry with the deep, rich, reduced flavors of slow-cooked meat. A dish like *Basteeya* (page 237) works best when it pushes the balance of sweet and savory right up to the edge.

Salt and Acid

Cumin, ginger, mustard, coriander, turmeric, saffron, and paprika are the principal spices that round out the mix, balancing the sweet spices with brighter, more salt-friendly and acid-friendly flavors. Turmeric, saffron, and paprika add bright color as well. Poultry and fish dishes, like Chicken Legs with Preserved Lemons and Green Olives (page 247), rely heavily on this family of spices.

Pepper and Heat

Moroccan food is seldom blazingly hot, tending more toward a pleasant tingle that complements other flavors than a fiery burn that obscures them. White and black peppercorns and cayenne are the most common sources of spicy heat in Moroccan cooking. Most of the cooks I know prefer white pepper over black, because they think it gives a finished dish a more refined appearance and more subtle flavor. Long pepper, a flavorful, floral pod, also turns up in spice blends and braises. And in my kitchen, I use two exceptionally flavorful Turkish peppers, Marash and Urfa (see page 32).

The Whole Story

Two decades ago, when I started trying to teach myself Moroccan cooking in the United States, I did what most people do: I rounded up some cookbooks and headed for the grocery store. Even back then, the spices I needed were right there on the shelf. For starters, I bought some ginger, turmeric, pepper, cumin, and coriander, and I began experimenting. Before long, the flavors started to taste like home, but something was missing. I began to realize that it was more a quality than a specific flavor. It was that mysterious fusion of aroma and taste that's everywhere in Moroccan food, and it's something you just can't quite get when you make Moroccan food with jars of supermarket spices.

Then one day, I wandered into an Indian grocery and dry goods store in Berkeley, and that was the moment everything changed. Everything in that store smelled like spices, even the scarves and tablecloths. Surrounded by bins and bags of the dried seeds and pods, roots, and chunks of bark I recognized from my childhood, I felt like I'd come home. *These* were the spices I needed. And ever since, I've been committed to buying spices whole and obsessive about grinding them fresh.

How obsessive? At our restaurant, we go through about half a pound of cumin seeds a day. But that doesn't mean that at the start of the shift a prep cook grinds half a pound of cumin seeds for everyone to use. Instead, each cook grinds only as much as he needs for whatever he's making. This is going to sound tyrannical, but I've actually fired

cooks for grinding enough spices to use over the course of several days as a shortcut. That's how big a difference I think it makes.

Of course, you don't have to be quite so obsessive at home. But my point is that grinding spices as you need them is not just some romantic foodie idea. Once you start grinding your own spices, you'll experience an immediate difference in their flavor and aroma.

I recommend that you make a (quite modest) investment in a spice grinder. Or buy an electric coffee grinder, the kind that looks like a mini-food processor—in which case, look for one with a stainless steel grinding well. Plastic wells tend to stain easily and absorb essential oils. Use this grinder only for spices. And here's a little trick that will surprise you. Right after you finish using your grinder, pulverize some stale bread in it to clean it and get rid of the residual oils. Pour out the bread and take a whiff of the grinder. Most, if not all, of the smell of the spices will be gone.

Some whole spices—notably ginger (as in big dried chunks of it), turmeric, and nutmeg—are rock hard and would probably ruin the blades or motor of your grinder. Grating them with a Microplane is a better plan. Cinnamon sticks can be either flaky and brittle or solid as a rock. Most can be ground in a spice grinder, but first, depending on how hard they are, pull them apart with your fingers, chop them into small pieces with a chef's knife, or fold a dish towel over them and smack them with the back of a frying pan to break them up. If none of these do the trick, grate the cinnamon with a Microplane.

There's another important reason to buy spices in whole form: you can toast them before grinding. Toasting ground spices doesn't work, because they burn too quickly, but toasting whole spices is quite easy to do and has an enormous effect on flavor and aroma. Think of the difference between a raw almond and a toasted almond, and you get the idea. The toasting is really an essential part of what makes us love the flavor of almonds, and the same goes for many spices. I'm fascinated by this transformation, and I've experimented with toasting all kinds of spices and other ingredients. I even tried toasting black peppercorns, which, I'm happy to tell you, makes their flavor more complex and mellow. Now I always toast them before grinding them or filling a pepper mill with them for the table.

The Life of Spice

Spices don't live forever. But if you store them whole in airtight containers away from heat, moisture, and light, they'll last longer. Sealing them with a vacuum food saver will also help. Once they're ground, their flavors and aromas start to deteriorate almost immediately. So, do what Moroccan cooks do: buy whole spices in small quantities, toast and grind only what you need, and store the rest whole and untoasted. And don't forget to label your spices with the date you bought them, so you can replace anything that gets too old. Six months is my suggested expiration date for whole spices (especially since you don't know how long they were sitting in the store before you bought them). A year is sometimes okay, but I wouldn't push it any further. In general, spice blends tend to last a bit longer than individual ground spices because once several spices are combined, deterioration of the overall flavor of the blend will be less noticeable.

Where do you get whole spices? Start by looking for a spice and herb company in your city, or check out Asian, Latin, and Indian grocery stores. If there's nothing like that where you live, befriend some local chefs and ask them where they get their stuff. And if that doesn't work, see the list of online and mail-order sources on page 380.

As a general rule, when I call for a ground spice in a recipe in this book, assume that I'm talking about spices you bought whole, toasted, and ground fairly recently (ideally, right before you started preparing that recipe), not store-bought preground spices. Of course, if that's all you have, go for it. But the flavors and aromas won't be as lively and exciting. In other words, think of spices as a spectrum, just as you would coffee: the closer you get to well-sourced, well-stored, well-toasted, and freshly ground, the better.

Cumin: A Mind-Bending Moment

You're undoubtedly familiar with cumin, one of the world's most recognizable spices. It shows up in everything from Indian curries to Tex-Mex chili to Middle Eastern dishes. It's also one of the most common spices in the Moroccan kitchen—and so essential that you'll often see little bowls of salt and cumin on a Moroccan table.

Now, you may love cumin, like I do, or you may be one of those people I meet all the time who wrinkle their nose and tell me that they've never been a fan. But either way, here's what I want you to understand: cumin is not the powder in that jar labeled "cumin" in your spice cabinet. That's *stale* cumin. I wouldn't blame you for not liking it. Throw it away before you read another word.

Buy some whole cumin seeds from a good source and toast and grind them (see page 30).

Pour that brown powder into a little bowl. Notice a difference? See how it's fluffy and slightly moist from the oil in the seeds? Smell the complex aroma? Now try sprinkling a little kosher salt and a bit of this freshly ground cumin on whatever you're having for dinner—a piece of chicken, fish, or meat. I promise you, you'll experience the flavor of cumin in a way that will amaze you. And salt and cumin might just become your new salt and pepper.

CUMIN SALT

Combine ¼ cup (30.6 grams) freshly toasted and ground cumin with 2 tablespoons (18 grams) kosher salt. Serve in small bowls at the table for sprinkling on, well, just about anything.

MAKES 6 TABLESPOONS (50 GRAMS)

Ras el Hanout

The most fundamental, defining flavor and aroma of Moroccan cooking comes from the country's "national spice blend," *ras el hanout*. The idea is much like curry powder. It's a blend that has an instantly recognizable aroma and adds an unmistakable flavor. Certain spices are always in it. Cumin and coriander take the lead, supported by sweet spices like cinnamon and nutmeg, and usually a fairly mild level of heat from a combination of peppers and chiles. But, just like curry powder, there is no single recipe for *ras el hanout*. You might even say that's its whole point.

The name means "head of the shop," or "top of the shop," and in a Moroccan market, every spice merchant sells his own signature blend, which you can buy either as a mix of whole spices to grind at home or ground to order.

There's a great deal of competition among shopkeepers about whose version has the most and the rarest stuff in it, with claims ranging to upwards of 175 ingredients. Although many cuisines have their spice blends—like Ethiopian *berbere,* Egyptian *duqqa,* and Cajun blackening seasoning—as far as I know, *ras el hanout* is the only one that has experienced this degree of out-of-control ingredient escalation.

In Marrakesh, there's really one place to buy spices: the old Jewish section of the medina called the *mellah*. That's where all the good spice merchants are. There are hardly any of them in the rest of the city, and anyone who cares about cooking still makes a trip to the *mellah* for spices. The merchants sell such high volumes that you can be sure you're always getting the freshest stuff.

Not long ago, I spent a couple of days hanging out with a guy I know only as Naser, the *ras* of one of these Marrakesh spice shops. I bought some of his ground *ras el hanout,* and, as I smelled and tasted it, I took notes while he rattled off a detailed accounting of its seventy-plus ingredients.

The next day, I went back and bought some of the same mix in whole form. I counted around twenty spices. I asked him where a few of the obvious missing elements were—the gum arabic, the grains of paradise. Naser looked around and then leaned in. "My friend," he said, "that recipe I told you . . . , well, . . . that's what I would make for myself at home. My ideal. My perfect recipe. This is what I sell here." In other words, of all the ingredients in *ras el hanout,* mystique remains perhaps the most important one.

The Stash

Serious Moroccan home cooks make their own personal *ras el hanout* blends, buying spices and toasting, grinding, and mixing them at home, often in secret. It's a custom that undoubtedly came out of the tradition of women working as cooks for royalty and wealthy families. Their signature spice blend was more than a matter of pride—it was their job security.

Recently, while sitting on the kitchen floor of my Aunt Samira's house in Marrakesh, I overheard the following interchange with her best friend, Souad, who was helping her make a seafood *basteeya*.

"Where's your *k'meesa?*" Souad asked.

Samira narrowed her eyes and stared at Souad for a moment before replying in a half-whisper, "It's on the top shelf of that cupboard, in back, in a bowl, inside a paper bag." She looked around and then added, "Wrapped in a sweater."

I've watched many a Moroccan woman at work in her kitchen, and when it comes time to add spices, the cooks I respect will invariably reach into a pocket or a cupboard and add a handful of their secret house spice blend, their homemade *ras el hanout,* or as it's slangily known, their *k'meesa,* or stash.

They'll let you watch them cook, they'll let you

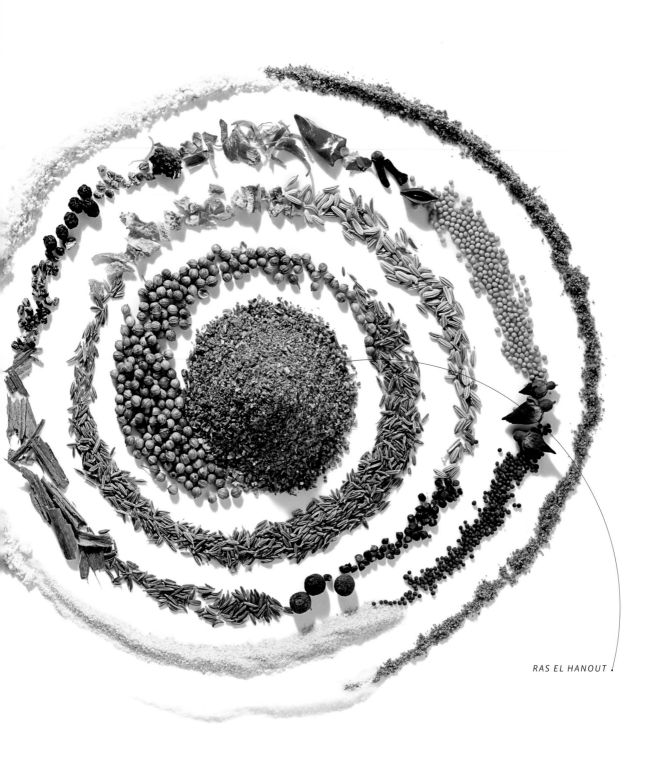

RAS EL HANOUT

see what ingredients they're adding, what techniques they're using, and what other spices they're throwing in, but the exact blend of the private stash is nobody's business but their own.

Where do I stand on all of this? I think 175-ingredient blends are overkill. You can't possibly taste so many spices all at once, and at some point, they start canceling each other out. And I don't see the point of secrets in cooking, since no two batches of spice are ever alike—and besides, my blend is constantly changing.

At the restaurant, we actually make five different *ras el hanout* blends for very specific uses. But what I want to share with you here is a really great all-purpose version I've come up with over the years, and a red variation that's particularly good with poultry and fish. This version contains the essential spice pantry of Morocco, with the exception of saffron, turmeric, paprika, and white pepper, and once you stock up on the ingredients, you'll have all of those individual spices to cook with.

It'll take some sleuthing to find the whole spices and a little work to put it all together. But in the end, you'll have your own *k'meesa*—your secret stash that you can use in recipes throughout this book (and hide in a sweater between uses). This first little exercise might even get you to clean out your spice rack and start thinking about spices in a new way.

RAS EL HANOUT

GATHERING AND MEASURING: This is the part that might take a while, because you may have to order some of the ingredients. Start by weighing or measuring the ingredients. In case you don't have a scale (yet), I've also provided teaspoon and tablespoon measures.

whole spices to be toasted: Weigh or measure these and put them in a medium heavy frying pan or cast-iron skillet:

3 tablespoons (11.4 grams) coriander seeds
1½ tablespoons (11.1 grams) cumin seeds
2 teaspoons (3.2 grams) dried orange peel
1¾ teaspoons (3.2 grams) fennel seeds
1 teaspoon (2 grams) grains of paradise
14 (2 grams) allspice berries
½ teaspoon (1.7 grams) caraway seeds
One 1½-inch piece (1.7 grams) cinnamon stick, crumbled
10 (1.6 grams) green cardamom pods, shelled and seeds reserved
½ teaspoon (1.5 grams) Tellicherry peppercorns
2 (1.5 grams) black cardamom pods, shelled and seeds reserved
1½ (1.3 grams) long peppers
¾ teaspoon (1.3 grams) whole mace
1 (0.6 gram) chile de árbol
8 (0.6 gram) cloves
½ (0.5 gram) star anise

whole spices you won't toast: Weigh or measure these and put them in a bowl:

1⅛ teaspoons (4.0 grams) yellow mustard seeds
2 teaspoons (1.9 grams) dried rosebuds
½ teaspoon (1.8 grams) brown mustard seeds

ground spices: Weigh or measure these and stir them together in a separate bowl:

1¾ teaspoons (5.6 grams) granulated garlic
2¼ teaspoons (4.6 grams) grated dried ginger (use a Microplane)
½ nutmeg (2.6 grams), grated (about 2½ teaspoons)
½ teaspoon (2.6 grams) citric acid